Simple Printmaking

Simple Printmaking

Relief and collage printing
Cyril Kent
Screen printing
Mary Cooper

Studio Vista London

Watson-Guptill Publications New York

General Editor Jean Richardson
© Cyril Kent & Mary Cooper 1966
Published in London by Studio Vista Limited
Blue Star House, Highgate Hill, London N19
and in New York by Watson-Guptill Publications
165 West 46th Street, New York 10036
Library of Congress Catalog Card Number 67-10436
Set in Folio Grotesque 8 and 9 pt.
Printed in the Netherlands
by N.V. Grafische Industrie Haarlem

Contents

Relief block printing

The technique of relief block printing is the simplest and most certainly the earliest method employed by man as a means of producing a printed image, and dates back in China to the 6th century A.D. Unlike certain later and more complex techniques which were developed, such as etching, lithography, etc., relief printing is an extremely basic and direct method, as anyone who has taken a rubbing from the surface of a coin will have discovered, though possibly at the time they may not have been aware of the association.

The design is effected by cutting away, or lowering by some other means, parts of the original surface of the material from which the print or impression is to be taken. Any material can be used, providing it is firm enough to withstand the pressure required to take an impression either with a press or by hand.

An impression can be taken in one of two ways - (a) by placing a sheet of paper over the relief image and rubbing over the surface with a soft pencil or wax crayon, or (b) by covering the surface or raised parts of the relief image with a film of printing ink, placing a sheet of paper over it, applying pressure and transferring the ink to that side of the paper in direct contact with the image, so producing a print.

1 Materials

Throughout its long history, wood has been the principal material used for producing relief blocks. For what are generally termed wood cuts, a knife and various shaped gouges are used on the grain side or plank of softer woods, e.g. cherry, pear, maple, American white wood, etc. (see fig. 4); whereas for wood engraving, which I shall deal with briefly later, the end or cross grain surface is used for engraving on, and harder and closer grained woods such as box, holly, etc. are used (see fig. 32).

Wood blocks specially prepared for cutting may be purchased type high (approximately $\frac{7}{8}''$ thick) but these work out rather expensive, and I would therefore recommend to the beginner certain alternative materials which are cheaper, and therefore more readily expendable, upon which to experiment in order to acquire and develop the necessary skill in the handling of the various tools. These alternative materials are linoleum and hardboard, both of which can usually be purchased as offcuts of a reasonable size quite cheaply.

Linoleum (lino)

This varies in thickness from about $\frac{1}{8}''$ to $\frac{1}{4}''$, the heaviest being known as cabin lino, which is particularly pleasant to work with. Linos of less than $\frac{1}{8}''$ tend to become rather unmanageable, especially if the design is large. Ordinary plain cork lino is the only suitable type for block cutting; inlaid lino will be found quite unsuitable. Old lino which has been well compressed with wear, providing the surface is in fair condition, will be found particularly pleasing to cut, being that much firmer. Before cutting, the lino may be mounted on to plywood or hardboard to give added support in cutting, but this is only necessary if the lino is thinner than $\frac{1}{8}''$ and therefore likely to distort if large areas are removed in the cutting.

Lino can be cut to the size required by cutting with a sharp knife on the canvas back. Once the canvas has been cut through, it will be found to break easily and cleanly. Should the lino appear hard and unpliable, slight warmth applied to the surface will soften the oil which it contains and make cutting easier.

Fig. 1 Rubbings taken from various objects and surfaces

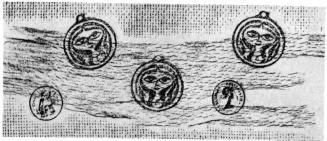

Hardboard

This is a material mainly designed for domestic construction-al purposes but for which many new uses have been found, not least of all by artists, many of whom use it in preference to canvas as a support for painting. For those interested in print making, it will also prove a very useful material. Hard-board, like lino, is a composition of even density and, similarly to lino, can be cut freely with the tools in any direction. It is produced in sheets of various sizes and thicknesses between about 3/32" to ¼", and is smooth on one side and textured on the other. Providing the tools used for cutting are sharp, quite crisp cutting is possible. There is, however, a tendency for the top surface to tear as the tool rises up from the cut. This, to some extent, can be obviated by first coating the surface thinly with ordinary gloss house paint and allowing it to dry before cutting. It should, however, be recognised that each material has its own inherent character which one should aim to exploit. In the case of both lino and hardboard, a bold, more open treatment is advisable, avoiding the use of fine lines left in relief which, owing to the relative softness of the material compared with wood, are apt to break down under pressure during printing.

Fig. 2 Section through a relief block showing knife and V cuts

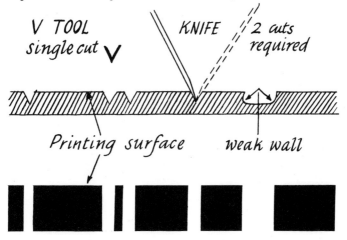

2 Tools and cutting

The knife

This is the tool principally used for wood cuts, but it can also be used as an alternative to, or in conjunction with, the V tool on softer materials such as those I have mentioned. To produce a white line with a knife, two cuts are required, the knife being held at an angle to the vertical and pulled towards the body, see fig. 2. If a black line is to be left in relief, four cuts will be required. In the hands of an experienced cutter, the knife is capable of producing very vigorous and fluent cutting and is especially well suited to large designs. To acquire such skill considerable practice is needed.

The V tool

This tool is appreciably easier to control than the knife. It is used for cutting round the main shapes as well as for creating textures of various kinds, as will be seen from the accompanying illustration (fig. 3a). The line produced will begin as a point, widening out according to the depth of cut and size of V tool used. Once the tool has reached a certain depth, it may be pushed forward to cut a line of even thickness. The width of the line will depend on how deeply the tool is buried.

10

Fig. 3 Cuts made with various tools (a) V tool (b) gouges. The ziz-zag line shown in the lower part is produced by rocking the gouge at a steep angle.

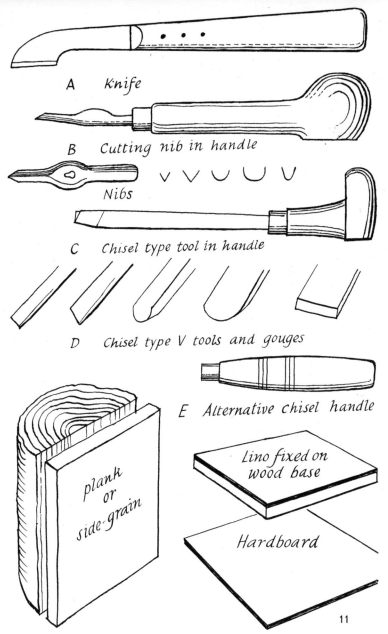

A Knife

B Cutting nib in handle

Nibs

C Chisel type tool in handle

D Chisel type V tools and gouges

E Alternative chisel handle

plank or side-grain

Lino fixed on wood base

Hardboard

11

Fig. 4 Tools for wood and lino cutting

The gouges

These which vary in both size and section are largely used for removing or lowering those parts of the material around the shapes and lines to be left in relief. Similar to the V tool, exciting textures can be effected with the various shaped gouges by holding the tools at different angles to the surface of the material when cutting. An interesting effect can also be achieved by rocking the gouge from side to side whilst cutting, see fig. 3(b).

As shown in fig. 4, it will be seen that both the V tools and gouges may be purchased in the nib or hollow chisel form, the latter being similar to those used for wood carving. The nibs are usually sold as a set containing two V tools, various shaped gouges and a handle, and will be found quite adequate for most work. The hollow chisel type tools are appreciably more expensive, but have a number of advantages. Firstly they are more rigid and considerably stronger than nibs. They are also easier and more satisfying to use, and can when necessary be reground and resharpened. Furthermore, they can be purchased in a wider variety of sizes in both V tools and gouges — a considerable advantage when dealing with large blocks.

The design

This is a subject on which one might write at considerable length, but there is not space for more than a brief appreciation of what I consider to be of particular importance in the design of a relief print.

In dealing with the single colour or black and white print, it is important to remember that in the absence of colour, the interest and excitement of the design will depend largely upon the way in which the solid areas of black and white are used in conjunction with the black and white line, with which the various greys and textures are produced.

You can learn a lot by studying the work of experienced artists, observing the manner in which certain effects are achieved and how each translates his or her ideas in terms of the media. The particular qualities of any medium, whether it is painting, sculpture or the various techniques of printmaking, must largely be subject to the materials and tools employed.

Each has its own particular language which one can only hope to discover through one's own personal experiments with the medium. In a relief print design (wood, lino, etc.), the character and relationship of shapes is of particular importance. It is a medium best suited to decorative treatment, and any attempt to deal with it in a strictly naturalistic manner is bound to prove a failure.

When making your design, work with as broad a medium as possible, e.g. brush and ink, chalk or charcoal. Avoid using a pencil, which forces one to think in terms of line rather than shape and pattern. Although the characteristic element of a relief print is the white line, your design will have greater richness if it also contains black line in parts. Textures, too, can be varied similarly by the use of white lines and shapes upon a dark ground, and vice-versa. One final point which I must emphasise is the need for personal experiment. By cutting directly into the material with the different tools, you will discover their natural characteristic shapes and marks. In this way, and in this way only, can one ultimately develop a true feeling and sympathy for one's medium.

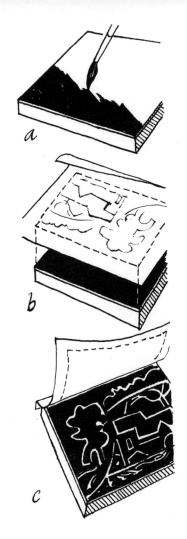

Fig. 5
(a) Preparing the block
(b) Tracing positioned on block
(c) Tracing removed to show design on block

13

Preparing the block (single colour)

Prior to cutting the block, it will generally be advisable to make some indication of the design on the block. For this purpose, I would suggest that you firstly coat the block with Indian ink or white poster colour. This will provide a more suitable ground on which to draw directly, or on which to trace the paper design. There is also an added advantage in using a ground of this kind when cutting, in that it makes it easier to see the lines and shapes created with the tools as the work progresses, the colour of the material acting as a contrast. (See fig. 5a.)

You may, if you feel confident enough, draw the design directly on the block, and I feel that one should be encouraged to do this on certain occasions as a means of developing a spontaneity of approach, so important to the creative act. If it seems a rather hazardous way of beginning, it is infinitely preferable to following slavishly a highly developed pencil drawing, allowing the tools little or no opportunity for expressing their individual character. As a general rule, it is better to express too little, rather than too much, when making a preparatory drawing on the block. When drawing directly on the block, one should bear in mind that when cut, the block will print in reverse. If you want it to print the same way round as drawn, a tracing will have to be made from your drawing. For this you will need a piece of tracing paper slightly larger than your design. This should be pinned down over your drawing or fixed with Scotch tape, leaving about 1" extending above the design. If the block has been treated with a coat of Indian ink, powdered white chalk should be rubbed into the tracing, the surplus chalk shaken off, and the tracing reversed down on to the block and fixed by turning the extra width of tracing paper to the back of the lino, wood or hardboard, and taping it down. (See fig. 5b.)

The tracing is now made with a ball pen or hardish pencil over the whole of the drawing, or over certain lines only, which one selects as a guide to the design. On removing the traced design, a white line will be seen on the black ground over those parts that have been traced through. (See fig. 5c.)

Ordinary carbon paper as used for typing can be used on a light ground for tracing through, and the coated side placed down on to the block.

14

Cutting the block

In order to control the tools properly, it is important that the table or bench used to work at is of a comfortable height. This will usually be found most satisfactory if slightly higher than the normal domestic table. It will also be an advantage if the block to be cut is placed on a suitable sized board, then put on the table and raised up two or three inches at the far end with a book or similar object. This will help to bring the work closer to you and provide a more comfortable angle for working.

During the process of cutting, the block is not held stationary but is moved and rotated according to the needs of the cutter. This is especially the case when dealing with curved lines, the block being turned and twisted in the direction of the cutting tool which is pushed through the material. The depth of cut can be varied in order to produce different thicknesses of line. The V tool and knife are mainly used for cutting round the contours of the shapes, because both these tools are capable of producing a stronger wall round the forms and lines which are to be left in relief; thus they are less likely to break down under pressure. (See fig. 2.)

Fig. 6 Cutting with V tool

Fig. 7 Clearing with gouge

Fig. 8 Turning block when cutting curves

15

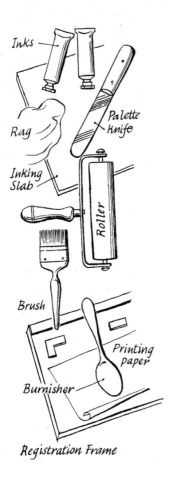

Inks

Rag

Palette knife

Inking Slab

Roller

Brush

Printing paper

Burnisher

Registration Frame

Fig. 9 Tools and equipment for printing

The method of holding the tools is shown in figs. 6-8. The depth of cut required in order to vary the weight of the white line is achieved by entering the lino or wood at a steeper angle with the tool. Once the correct depth has been reached, the tool can then be levelled off and pushed through the material to produce a line of even width.

When cutting, only the thumb of the hand controlling the tool is in direct contact with the surface of the block, so allowing greater freedom of movement in the cutting. The rotating of the block is done with the left hand, turning it in whatever direction the line is intended to go. At first some difficulty may be experienced in visualizing the results of your cutting, and you will no doubt feel the need to take trial proofs fairly frequently during the process of cutting the block. As you gain experience, you will find that it will become easier to see what you have cut in terms of black and white.

Having used the V tool or knife to cut round those parts of the design sufficiently to define the main shapes, a print can now be taken. Once the main disposition of the black and white areas has been decided on, the white shapes should be removed with the gouges. In order to ensure that the inked roller will not reach parts within the shapes intended to print white, make certain that the material is cut back deeply enough. In the case of lino, any large areas should be cut down to the canvas backing. In the early stages, however, do not worry unduly about this. Unintentional effects of this kind can often be interestingly exploited during the later cutting stages.

Fig. 10 Rollers in stand

The final stages will now be principally concerned with developing the tone and textural interest of the print, using the V tool, knife and various gouges. Tones are produced by the use of lines and dots or marks of various kinds which are made by using the tools in different ways. For example, fine white lines openly spaced will produce a relatively dark tone, compared with a series of thick white lines which have been closely cut. Similarly, different sized dots or marks will produce textures of different tonal values according to their size and spacing.

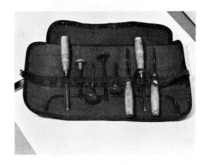

Fig. 11 Tools in roll-up bag

Inking slabs

These are used for rolling the ink on prior to inking the block. The material used is not important providing it is firm, smooth and of a nonporous nature. Plate-glass sheets can be bought in various sizes, but heavy gauge window glass will do quite well if the edges

Fig. 12 Inking-up slab

Fig. 13 Three colour lino-cut design - see figs 20, 21 and 22

Fig. 14 Inking-up the block

Fig. 15 Taking a proof, burnishing with spoon

are bevelled off with a file. 10″ x 8″ will be found a good size. Alternatively, hardboard, plastic or metal sheet can be used. If you use glass, place a piece of white paper beneath it in order to help you see your colour better. White plastic sheet can be bought mounted on hardboard, and cut to size it will make excellent inking slabs. If you are using colour, you will need at least three of these.

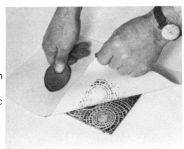

Fig. 16 Inspecting proof

Papers for printing

Much of the quality of a print depends on the character of the paper used. For example, smooth, hard-surfaced papers will give very dense black or colour and sharp contours to the forms, producing a less subtle print than is possible on softer, more absorbent papers. You therefore need to consider carefully your choice of paper with regard to the design.

For your first experiments, however, quite cheap papers can be used, e.g., thin cartridge and student grade drawing papers of varying surfaces, tissues and common newsprint will be found perfectly adequate.

Fig. 17 Linocut, first stage: white line only

Fig. 18 Linocut, second stage: larger areas of white removed

Fig. 19 Final print

Rollers

The rollers used for transferring the ink from the slab to the surface of the block can be purchased in various sizes from 1″ up to 7″ in width and between approx. 1″ and 2″ in diameter. The cheapest are made of rubber and are quite satisfactory. Composition rollers will last infinitely longer, but are considerably more expensive. A simple stand constructed of wood in which the rollers can be placed when not in use is shown in fig. 10.

Palette knives

These are required for spreading the ink on to the inking slab and for mixing colours. One will be sufficient, but when using colour, you will find it an advantage to have more. A knife with a blade 5″ to 6″ long will prove a convenient size.

Brush

This is not essential, but will be found very useful for cleaning the block of loose chippings before printing. An ordinary, cheap, decorating type between 1½" and 2" wide will do.

Burnisher

Any suitably hard surface that is curved and smooth can be used as a burnisher, e.g., the bowl of a wood pipe or a wood or metal spoon. By rubbing it over the back of the print when in place on the block, varying density of black or colour can be produced depending on the amount of pressure applied.

Printing inks

Special oil or water-based inks can be bought in tubes or tins for block printing, but colours used for oil painting can also be used, though some colours will be found a little difficult to roll up. Oil colour printing inks are of a pleasanter consistency for rolling up than water-based inks, and as a rule can be obtained in a wider range of colours. Owing to the oil, finer glazes of colour are also possible than can be obtained with watercolours. If the colour appears too thick or tacky, a few drops of turpentine or turps substitute will thin it to the required consistency. This can also be used for cleaning up the slabs, rollers, etc.

Water-based inks, on the other hand, may be more convenient to use and require only a little water to thin them. Water is used as a solvent when cleaning up. Certain water-based colours will appear to have greater luminosity than their counterparts in oil, and you will be well advised to experiment with both in order to discover more fully the qualities of each. Oil and water colours should never be mixed, but oil colours will print quite satisfactorily over watercolours.

Rag

You will need a plentiful supply of old cotton rags or net curtaining for cleaning the slabs, blocks and rollers, etc.

Fig. 20: Red block

Figs 20-22 show colour blocks
used for 3 colour linocut in
fig. 13. Fig. 21 was used as the
key block.

Fig. 21: Green block

Fig. 22: Yellow ochre block

Inking the block

Preparatory to printing, cut your printing paper to a suitable size — if using a single colour block, a margin of roughly 1″ all round the block will be sufficient. Now place some newspaper or newsprint on your table or bench to protect it from any stray ink. Place your ink slab on this and squeeze your colour on to it. After a little experience you will find it easier to estimate just how much ink to put down for the required job, depending as it will on the size of your print and the number to be taken. With the palette knife spread the ink in a line across the top of the plate to roughly the width of your roller. Using the roller, work the ink out evenly over the slab. When the right amount of ink has been used ,the roller should have a thin smooth coat of ink evenly distributed over its surface.

Having inked up the roller, place the cut block on the table next to your ink slab and distribute the ink evenly over the surface by moving the roller along the block, and then across it, until you are satisfied that all the raised parts of your block have been covered with an equal weight of ink.

Fig. 23 Hardboard cut - landscape

3 Printing

To print your block, place it on a clean sheet of paper to ensure that the edges of the print are not soiled by stray ink on the table. Place your printing paper over it, as centrally as possible, and with the palm of the hand and working from the centre of the block to the sides, press the paper out firmly on to the surface, avoiding creases of any kind.

If the printing paper is very thin, it will be possible to see quite clearly the inked areas of your block through it, and even with thicker papers a certain amount of the ink absorbed will help you to see a fairly clear image.

To complete the proof, rub over the back of the paper with your burnisher, varying the degree of pressure in those parts where less density of colour is required. (See fig. 15.) The paper can be lifted at the corners during this process to examine the state of the print (fig. 16). Having taken a proof, fresh consideration can now be given to what further cutting is required. The work should progress in this way through alternating stages of cutting and printing, until the final proof has been taken.

Colour printing

The nature of the preliminary paper design will very largely depend on what information is felt to be necessary as a guide to the cutting. In certain cases little more than a very broad and free indication of the shapes and colour arrangement may be required. On the other hand, if the idea is more complex, you will need a more elaborate colour design. But, once again, I would remind you that the paper design should only serve as a guide — once the cutting of the first block has begun, the tools and the material must be given freedom to suggest the character of the treatment.

Use a brush and colour to prepare your paper design, or a similarly broad medium such as crayon or chalk. Waterproof colour inks will be found very useful, as they are very transparent and give a fairly true indication of what may be achieved in the overprinting of your colours in the print.

Fig. 24 Linocut - still life

Preparing the block

Having made your paper design and decided on the number of colours you want to use, the blocks can now be prepared, one for each colour. Before cutting them you will need to decide on what method you will use to ensure the correct registration of your colours; in other words, how you will locate your print on each of the separate colour blocks, so that the colours will print in their correct relationship to one another.

An easy, if not entirely foolproof, method is shown in fig. 25a. An allowance is made when cutting the blocks to size, of roughly 1½″ on the top and left-hand edges, to act as a margin to the print and as a means of locating it. This method has certain disadvantages, particularly when inking up the blocks, as ink can very easily stray into the margin, and unless care is taken to wipe the edges of the block clean before printing, the print can be spoiled.

The method I would advocate is the use of a simple registration frame (shown in fig. 25(b) and constructed from a ¼" piece of plywood or an old drawing board) to act as a base, and a few pieces of lino or hardboard to serve as guides in positioning the block and the printing paper. The particular advantages of the registration frame are that the blocks need only be cut to the size of the design, and secondly, a more foolproof method of registering the paper is possible, as will be seen.

The blocks can be cut to size according to the method you decide to use. Make sure that the top and left-hand edges are as squarely cut as possible; this is most important, otherwise you will fail to get proper registration. The surface of the blocks should now be darkened with Indian ink or a thin coat of black poster colour, and put aside to dry.

The use of a key block

Although, as I have said earlier, each colour block should be used as fully as possible to develop the form of your design, it will usually be found that one of the colours used gives a clearer reference to the various shapes and their ar-

Fig.25 Methods of registering colour print: (a) showing printing paper located on block (b) use of simple registration frame

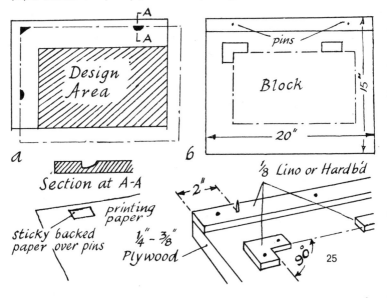

25

rangement within the design than any of the other colours. This will be the colour block that will act as a key to your other colours and should be cut first. Which of the colours is chosen is of no importance providing it gives reference to the shapes.

Now make a tracing of your paper design to provide the information necessary as a guide to the cutting of your first colour - the key block. Use a somewhat larger sheet of tracing paper for this than will cover the block, allowing a margin of 2″ approximately all round, so that it can be folded back behind the block when transferring your tracing on to it. Trace your design through on to the block, remembering to reverse the tracing before doing so to ensure that your design will finally print the correct way round.

Before beginning the cutting, you may find it a help, particularly if the design is rather complicated, to fill in with chalk or white poster colour the areas of your key block colour to be left in relief. Remember, however, that as this block is to act not only as a colour within the design but also initially as a guide to the remaining colours, it will be as well to leave slightly more to print in the early stages, so that the fullest reference possible is given to the arrangement of the main shapes. Those parts not required can be cut away later.

The cutting of your key block can now be done, using the V tool or knife to cut round those parts of the shapes where a firm boundary to the colour is required, followed by the use of the gouges for removing those areas which you have decided you do not wish to print either as a pure colour or in overprintings with your other colours. When you have cut away as much of the key block as you feel necessary as a guide to the design, a print can be taken from it and transferred on to the surfaces of the remaining colour blocks, using the registration frame or the alternative method.

If a registration frame is used, the printing paper should be cut to size, allowing at least a 2″ margin all round your block. A thin, printing tissue paper will prove most suitable for this purpose, as it is important that as little ink as possible should be absorbed into the paper. Place the paper over the registration frame so that it covers the location pins, making sure an equal margin of paper is left to the sides and base of your block. The paper can now be pressed over the pins and reinforced at these points with a small

Fig. 26 Linocut - white line only

square of brown, sticky-backed paper or Scotch tape to prevent the paper tearing (fig. 25).

The block should now be inked up for the single block print. As the print will have to be transferred down on to the surface of your other blocks as a guide to the cutting, it will need to be inked up fairly heavily in white or a suitably light colour, so that when offset on to the darkened surface of the blocks it will show clearly. With the printing paper firmly fixed on the pins of the frame and thrown back, place the inked key block in the correct position and bring the paper down on to it, smoothing it out over the block with the side of the hand, working from the top downwards and out to the sides.

With a clean roller finish taking your print. Run it over the whole area, using a fair amount of pressure so as to

Fig. 27 Hardboard cut - abstract use of line and textures

remove as much of the ink from the surface as possible. Lift the print at each corner to make sure that a good, clear impression has been taken; if not, place it down again and continue with the roller. When you are satisfied that a heavy enough print has been taken, lift the print from the block, still keeping it on the pins, and drop it back clear of the block.

The key block can now be removed and your second block placed in the same position in the registration frame. The print is now placed down on to it and once again, by using the roller, an image of your key print will be transferred to the surface. The same procedure is followed for transferring the print to your other blocks. If the print of your key block was sufficiently heavy, at least three or four impressions, or offsets, should be possible. Should more be required, a fresh print can be taken.

Once the blocks have been allowed to dry, the cutting for your second colour can begin. As in the case of the key block, cut no more away than is really necessary, and leave as much as possible to print in the early stages. It is always advisable to refrain from cutting colour areas away should there be any doubt in your mind, as mistakes cannot be easily remedied once they have been made.

Should your key block fail to give sufficient reference to certain parts of the design, your tracing can be used to supply this, by placing it down on to the block and drawing through. Furthermore, a print from your second block can be taken and transferred, using a different colour, on to your subsequent third and fourth blocks, etc., if you feel it necessary. Or again, further drawing done on the back of a key block print can be traced through with blue carbon paper.

Once the initial cutting of all your blocks has been done, a series of progressive prints may be taken, using the registration frame as described for your key block print. A number of sheets of printing paper should be prepared for this purpose.

Ink up your separate colour blocks, making sure beforehand to brush any loose chippings off the surface and out of the grooves. Mix up your colours as carefully as possible and experiment by printing the blocks in varying sequence, e.g., the block used for your key may be printed first, followed by the second and third, etc. printed one over another in their order of cutting. This order of printing may give you the results you want, depending on the colours and their tone and transparency. But you will need to experiment, particularly in the later stages of printing, to arrive at the most satisfactory colour and the order in which they should be printed.

By working in this manner and allowing the effects of your colour overprintings to suggest each fresh stage of the cutting, the work becomes truly creative rather than a slavish method of reproducing a paper design. Each fresh print pulled is an exciting adventure, as one is never entirely sure of the total effect until it is peeled from the last colour block. With experience in the overprinting of your colours, you will soon come to know how colours behave, and how to achieve the most satisfactory results from the order in which they are printed.

Fig. 28 Single block colour print

Colour printing using a single block

This method, sometimes referred to as the 'waste method' and advocated by John Newick in Making Colour Prints (Dryad, London), is done on a single block. With this, the cutting is done in a series of stages between printings, removing more of the block each time so that only small areas remain to print the final colour.

As a method of working it has much to recommend it, particularly as a means of developing clear thinking in the design stage and a spontaneity of approach in cutting. It has, however, certain limitations.

Unlike the method of colour printing in which separate blocks are used for the colours, the order of printing the colours with a single block is restricted, and all the printings for each colour have to be taken between the cutting stages in a particular order.

Fig. 29 1st colour, ochre, only areas to print white removed

Fig. 30 2nd colour, grey, printed over ochre after further cutting

Fig. 31 3rd colour, dark blue, printed over ochre and grey after further cutting

Figs 29-31 show the various stages in developing a print of this kind. In fig. 29, only those areas of the print which are required to remain white have been removed. Fig. 30 shows further parts of the block removed to produce other shapes and lines etc. to print over fig. 29. The final shapes left to print over figs 29 and 30 as a final colour are shown in fig. 31.

Wood engraving

Within the limits of this book, it is not possible to do more than give a brief description of this most delightful and intriguing medium. For those wishing to acquaint themselves more fully regarding the technique, a list of books is given on page 95.

Wood engraving as a medium differs from the wood and linocut only in the materials and tools that are employed; basically the same procedure is adopted for the cutting and printing. Like the wood and lino-cut, it is a relief method, the print being taken from the raised surface after engraving.

As we have seen, for the cut design for which relatively soft materials are used, the cutting is done with hollow type 'V' tools and gouges, whereas for wood engraving, harder and more compact materials such as box, holly etc., are used and the design engraved upon them with specially designed tools (see fig. 32). The graver, or burin as it is called, is similar to that used in metal engraving.

The principal difference in the appearance of a wood

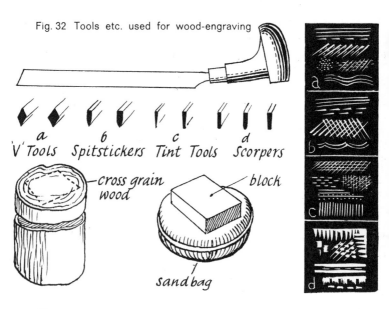

Fig. 32 Tools etc. used for wood-engraving

a   b   c   d
V Tools   Spitstickers   Tint Tools   Scorpers

cross grain wood   block

sand bag

Fig. 33 Collage · print

Fig. 34 Holding the engraving tool

Fig. 35 Engraving

engraving print is the greater delicacy of treatment, made possible by the use of harder materials and by the finer nature of the engraving tools used.

Unfortunately blocks specially prepared for the purpose are expensive, and the beginner who feels keen to try his hand at wood engraving would be well advised to gain his experience on less precious materials. Plastics of various kinds can be used to engrave on. Vinyl of the kind used for floor tiling in 9″ squares, approx. 1/16″ thick, gives excellent results. Owing to the thinness of these materials, they need to be mounted on a piece of plywood or thicker hardboard.

Fig. 36
Wood engraving

Collage prints

A collage print may briefly be described as an impression taken from the surfaces of various materials which have first been fixed down upon a base before inking up, or inked separately and placed down upon the printing surface. It is in fact another method of relief printing using a raised surface. The difference is that whereas in the cut or engraved design the artist is limited as regards the effects he can produce by his tools and materials, in the collage design there is no such restriction. For here you do not cut or create your own textures, you extract them from whatever source you have to hand, allowing the materials freedom to actively direct and stimulate your thoughts.

The materials used in a collage print may be drawn from many sources; any surface which it is possible to ink up with a roller and which is sufficiently firm to take an impression from, may be made to play a useful role. The varied examples of collage designs which I have used to illustrate this brief description, have all been created with the use of such scraps of commonplace materials as one might find rummaging through an old drawer, garden shed or on a stroll through the fields or woods.

Nature offers a rich source for collage design. The great variety of shapes and vein structures to be found in leaves, the wonderful surface patterns of wood grains and other natural forms of the fields and country lanes provide exciting materials for anyone who is prepared to look. If we add to this, the very wide range of synthetic materials with interesting surface textures, especially in the field of plastics, and the various types of composition board used in building, you will begin to realise just how wide the range of materials is.

The following pages show examples of impressions taken from the surfaces of various materials, each possessing its own distinctive character. You will notice that when a number of different textures are seen together in this way, their particular qualities become more evident by reason of contrast. Fine delicate textures such as those obtained from a piece of muslin or fine cotton material, when used together with coarser textures such as hessian (burlap), rough canvas or crumpled newspaper, give added interest to each other. It is this play upon the textural quality of the various materials that will be largely responsible for the variety and excitement of your design.

4 Materials

Natural forms

These have provided a constant course of inspiration to the artist and craftsman throughout the ages. By observing and studying the innumerable forms and growth patterns in nature, a deeper understanding and awareness of the meaning of design is acquired. Leaves, grasses, feathers, wood grains of every description, and even dried flower heads and seed pods, each offer in their various ways unlimited possibilities for creating exciting patterns and as elements within the collage print.

Those who have not tried experimenting with repeat pattern will find among the forms in nature a great variety of material offering exciting shapes and textures with which to create designs. By organising them in various ways you will discover how different rhythms are developed. Using colour, an experiment of this kind can be extended in a variety of ways.

Natural forms contrasted with shapes cut or torn out of manufactured materials possessing quite different surface textures, can evoke moods of quite a subtle and poetic kind.

Apart from those forms in nature which have their own distinctive character or shape, there are others, such as wood grains, which we are mostly familiar with in plank form. Rhythms of this kind in the grain structure of old fence boarding, or fragments of boarding, broken and weathered so that the softer fibres which lie between the grain sink, present a wonderful surface from which to take an impression. Textures of this kind will be found extremely valuable in collage printing, both for their wonderful abstract qualities of rhythmic line, and for their power of association which suggests the currents of movement in water, wind and sky.

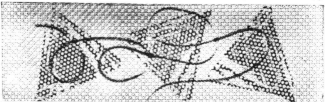

Fig. 37 Background texture taken from embossed chocolate box top, wire gauze shapes and string printed over

Fig. 38 Print taken from materials fixed down on hardboard base block. Materials include corrugated cardboard, crumpled tissue paper, embossed wallpaper, lace and cotton.

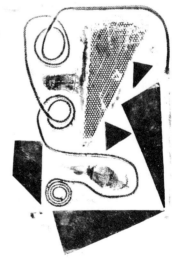

Fig. 39 String, wire gauze and cut cardboard shapes fixed to base block before printing

Paper and cardboard

Paper and cardboard of various thickness and surface texture play an indispensable part in the constructing of a collage print, and may often be used in all the various stages of assembling and printing. There are few other materials which differ so in their surface qualities.

Some of the most intriguing effects can be obtained from the thinnest and cheapest of papers, such as tissue and newsprint, by crumpling or folding them in various ways and fixing them on the base before printing. Paper textures vary from the most delicate granular surfaces, such as cartridge and other forms of drawing and watercolour papers, to the quite bold textures of the moulded or embossed papers, such as corrugated paper and wallpaper. All these, including even sweet wrapping papers and various types of foil, can be used in interesting ways to give textural interest.

Where areas of flat colour are required, shapes can be cut out of a smooth surfaced paper or from thin cardboard, fixed down upon a ground and inked up, or printed free, giving perfectly good results. Thicker cardboard, strawboard, chipboard and tougher, smooth surfaced materials, will be found more serviceable should you wish to move the shapes around so that they can be used more widely in the print, or in a number of prints, for the purpose of experiment.

Fabrics

Woven materials of every kind can be used to give wonderfully rich textures to a print, and like many natural forms, they have the power to evoke associations in a curious and enchanting way. Scraps can be used from old dress and curtain materials, net stockings, string vests, odd bits of upholstery and covering materials, such as hessian (burlap) and corduroy. Even knitted materials - string and cotton, etc. - will be found of service. There is, in fact, hardly an end to the textural qualities to be found in this field.

Certain materials, such as fine net and similar light woven fabrics, being very flexible, can be used to produce unique effects in their free, delicate folds. Owing to their lightness, however, they will tend to get picked up by the inked roller unless fixed down upon a ground prior to printing. Heavier and closer woven materials, such as hessian and certain

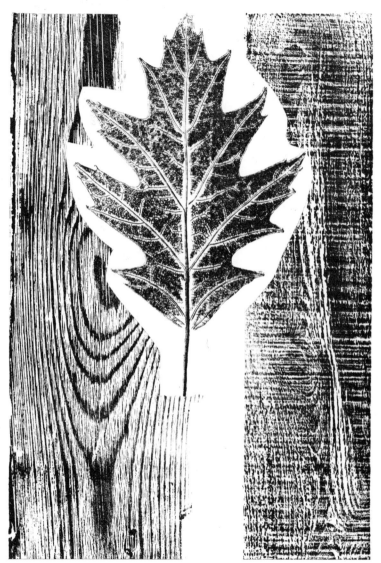

Fig. 40 Leaf and woodgrain prints

cottons, will suggest more static shapes because they produce more regular textures.

Materials of this kind present no problems as regards shaping them; scissors and a knife are all that you need. Remember, however, that the particular qualities of woven materials lie in their structure of overlapping strands. Allow the shapes to express this by exploiting the frayed edge of the material in certain cases.

It may be found difficult at first to ink up the heavier and more absorbent materials, but these will be less troublesome once the first coat of ink has dried in to form a seal.

Building materials

There are many new materials used in building construction today which possess interesting surfaces, especially among the various types of composition board and plastic materials. Hardboards of different kinds, some perforated, chipboard and a wide range of light insulation boarding can all contribute in a variety of ways to the collage print. These materials vary in thickness between $\frac{1}{8}''$ and $\frac{1}{2}''$ and can usually be purchased as offcuts of a convenient size quite cheaply.

Hardboards which are smooth on one side and textured on the other are thinner than insulation board but tougher, and require to be cut with a small tenon or fretsaw. Rolled up with ink the smooth side will print quite solidly, and apart from its use within the collage design, hardboard is excellent as a surface for rolling your inks up on. Used as a base, its textured side, which is of a rather mechanical nature, can act as a background inked up with other shapes which have been laid upon it. The perforated types of hardboard, on the other hand, have circular or rectangular cut outs which produce very bold effects. If used judiciously, they can be made to contribute most valuably to a print.

Insulation boards, though usually thicker than hardboard, are softer and can easily be cut with a sharp knife. Their surfaces, both of which are textured, are of a less regular character than hardboard. Like the hardboards, they will serve admirably as base blocks or as cut shapes within the collage.

Glass, of which there is a great variety of different patterned surfaces to be found on the market today, both of

Fig. 41 Leaf and feather prints

39

the rolled and moulded kind, offers very rich and exciting surfaces from which to print. A few examples are shown in fig. 46. Most glass merchants will be quite happy to let you have the odd strips and broken fragments for a small charge. These, used in strip form or as irregular shapes inked up and overprinted in various ways in black and colour, or used in combination with other materials, are capable of producing quite wonderful effects. Where solid areas of colour are required, plain glass may be similarly used. (See fig. 59.)

To overcome the difficulty of shaping glass and other equally hard materials, stencils may be used, as will be explained later.

Other materials worth investigating are chicken wire and metal gauze sheeting, both to be found in a variety of sizes and patterns. These may be shaped with tin snips or, as suggested above, controlled with the use of stencils.

I have dealt at some length on the subject of materials, yet I have only touched upon the more common and ready to hand surfaces with which a collage print may be made. It is for you to discover for yourselves and to experiment with all kinds of possible materials capable of contributing new and exciting qualities to your prints.

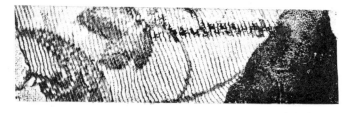

Fig. 42 Print taken from piece of open lace and torn paper fixed down on base

Opposite:
Fig. 43 Fabrics and paper (a) corduroy (b) rough canvas (c) embossed wallpaper (d) corrugated paper (e,f) lace (g) muslin

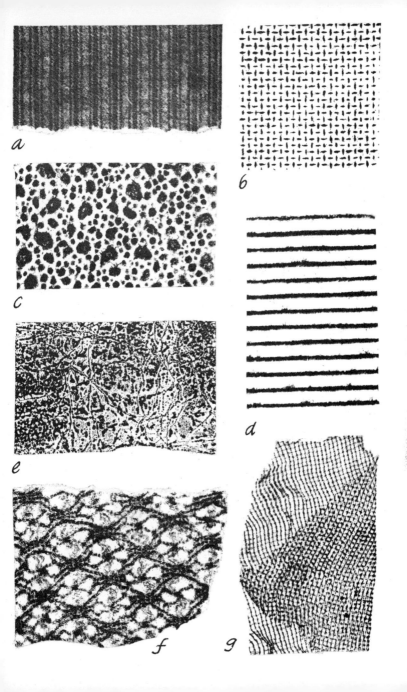

a

b

c

d

e

f

g

Fig. 44 Abstract design using direct method. The various materials were not fixed but inked up separately and placed down on to the printing paper. The background colour was taken from a rolled up piece of hadboard on which cotton was dropped before printing.

Fig. 45 Leaf print inked up and printed on plywood ground

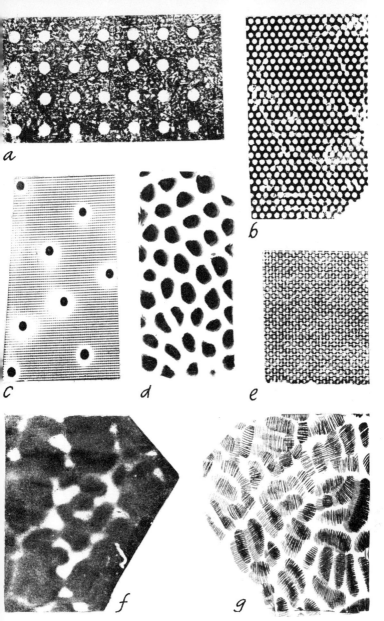

Fig. 46 Textures taken from building materials (a) perforated insulation board (b) wire gauze (c, d, f, g) textured glass (e) hardboard

5 Tools

To construct a collage design a very limited number of tools are required, most of which are usually to be found in the house or toolshed.

(1) Scissors
For cutting and shaping paper, thin cardboard and all forms of woven materials, a good sharp pair of scissors with a blade of not less than 4″ will be required.

(2) Knife
This will be found essential for dealing with heavier cardboard, certain of the softer insulation boards, and the thinner plywoods and veneers. A good sharp penknife will serve, but a stencil type cutting knife such as illustrated will amply justify the small outlay, as it is possible to exert greater pressure and is easier to control. The particular function of the knife is for the cutting of masks and stencils (figs. 61 and 62).

(3) Metal rule
A metal rule or straight edge is an indispensable part of one's equipment, for there are innumerable occasions when it is necessary to cut a straight edge to paper, cardboard etc., and although a wooden ruler or straight piece of hardwood may serve for cutting against, a metal rule is infinitely safer and easier to manage.

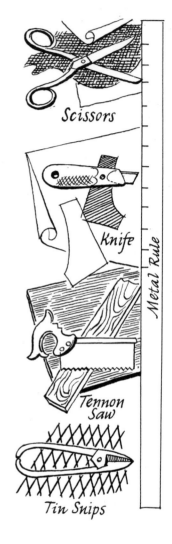

Fig. 47 Tools and equipment for collage printing

(4) Tenon saw

Although there will be few occasions when one will need this, it will be found indispensable for cutting wood planking and the tougher materials such as hardboard.

(5) Tin snips

Assuming that it would not strain your resources too much, I would suggest as a final item of equipment a small pair of tin snips for cutting wire mesh, metal gauze and the thicker tin foils.

(6) Adhesives

For fixing the various materials to a base block, rubber solution ('Cow gum') or any similar rubber based adhesive will be required.

You will also need some drawing pins (thumbtacks), and a roll of Scotch tape about ¾″ to 1″ wide, for fixing prints and masking strips.

With experience you will develop your own way of working, and will no doubt find the need to add other tools to this basic kit. Some you may adapt, others you will construct yourself, each to serve a particular purpose in one or other of the stages of print making. Some of the most effective tools used by craftsmen have been improvised from oddments which have been near at hand.

The collage design, by its very nature, demands greater flexibility in both the design as well as the printing stages. This calls for some ingenuity on the part of the artist, forcing him to seek for less conventional means of achieving his aims.

Tools and materials for printing

Being a relief method, the tools and materials used in collage printing are virtually the same as those described in the earlier section dealing with block printing in lino, wood, etc. You will need:

    (a) Rollers (of various sizes)
    (b) Inking slabs (at least 3 - glass, hardboard, etc.)
    (c) Palette knives (at least 2)
    (d) Inks (both water and oil-based inks)
    (e) Burnisher (bowl of spoon or similar surface)
    (f) Rag
    (g) Registration frame

With regard to printing papers, I would suggest that you experiment with as wide a variety as you can get hold of, from the cheapest newsprint to the heavier cartridge (drawing) papers. The harder, smooth surfaced papers will give a firmer image and denser colour, whereas the coarser the surface the softer and less solid the colour will be. By experimenting you will discover the qualities of each.

6 Designing a collage print

There are a number of ways in which collage can be used in constructing a design. The important point to remember is that if we are to exploit fully the true potentialities of the media, we must allow the materials full freedom to stimulate and direct our thoughts. This is essential to the nature of a collage print.

A print can develop in one of a number of ways: -

(a) The design may be very simple, composed of no more than one or two shapes, the interest in the print being achieved by the relationship of the shapes and textures, and of the colours if used; in other words, their pure formal qualities. Used in this way, shapes cut or taken as we find them in nature, for example, leaves and feathers, can be arranged and printed in various ways to produce interesting patterns. You will be well rewarded by experimenting in this way with different materials as a means of developing a sensitivity for the qualities of shape and texture.

(b) Having experimented freely as suggested above, let us imagine that we have gathered together a number of materials of various kinds which have interested us for their shape and surface textures. Having placed them on a table or on the floor, where we have a better opportunity of studying their individual qualities, we become aware of certain associations which these fragments touch off in our visual memory. Among the materials there will be those that have a direct association with each other - a piece of rough sacking, a length of string and a piece of weathered broken boarding - it will be these that will stimulate the idea initially. In this case, the idea suggested by these simple fragments may have to do with the sea shore or perhaps broken down farm sheds, dependent on one's own personal visual experiences. The idea itself is not important; what is important

Fig. 48 Collage block showing materials fixed to base block

Fig. 49 Print taken from above block

is that we should try to use and arrange the surface textures in an expressive way to evoke a particular mood.

(c) This process also works in reverse, so to speak. As we become more familiar with the effects that can be created with the materials, we shall begin to find ourselves translating our visual experiences in terms of shape, texture and colour arrangements. The pattern suggested in a ploughed field, seen in relation to the movements in trees and cloud forms, might be such an experience; or the strong shapes of cliffs seen against the sea and sky; or again perhaps a familiar experience such as the movements of birds in flight. One could go on suggesting further themes, but there is no need, provided I have made my point that materials can evoke ideas, and ideas can evoke materials.

Irrespective of how and in what way the idea may develop, the method or technique of both constructing and printing your design will be basically the same.

Fig. 50 Print taken from net material fixed to base block with the printing paper fixed at top of base block with drawing pins

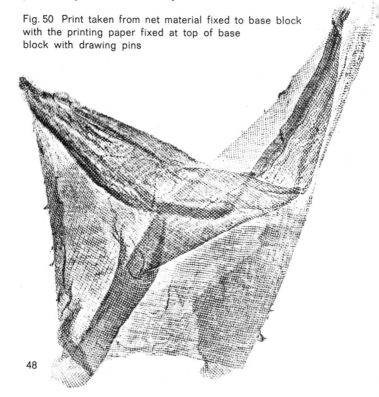

48

Fig. 51 With a print of fig. 50 fixed to base block, the above print was developed with the use of other materials and by rolling up with colour parts of base block. For key see fig. 52

Fig. 52 (1) Net shape (2) colour rolled up on base block to represent areas of sea and sky. Shape of quay and sun masked off with metal foil. Further shapes were then added including (3) embossed wallpaper (4) hessian (5) cut cardboard shapes.

49

7 Construction and printing

1 Using a base block

The base block may be cut from any material, provided it is sufficiently firm to hold or support the shapes fixed or placed down on it. Even thick paper or thin cardboard will be quite suitable. The size of such a base is largely a matter of personal convenience, subject to the space you have available for working and the nature of the design and materials used. For general use and experiment, a base of 15" x 20" will be found a pleasing proportion to work on. A base block can be made to play an important part in the process of constructing a collage design for the following reasons: -

(a) Cut to a suitable working size, it acts as a shape in which to arrange the different elements - an important function.

(b) Acting as a background to these forms, its surface texture can be usefully employed to give added interest and cohesion to the design.

Having chosen your base block, you can either fix the materials down on to it prior to inking up with the roller, as in fig. 48, or they can be inked up separately and placed down in the position required. Which of these methods you use will largely depend on the nature of the materials, e.g., light flexible materials, such as fine muslin, lace or paper shapes, will need to be fixed down before rolling up to prevent them from moving during the inking and printing stages. Heavier and stiffer materials can be inked up separately and placed down on the block together with the fixed shapes if one wishes, or printed at a later stage.

Rubber solution (rubber cement) or Copydex (casein glue) will be found quite adequate for fixing all woven type materials, cardboard and paper of all descriptions, and such natural materials as leaves, feathers and light veneered plywoods. Although they are not so suitable for metallic and non-porous materials such as wire mesh, glass and plastic, if sufficient time is allowed for the solution to dry (remembering to coat both surfaces), they will be found to hold these materials firmly enough in place to allow for printing. These adhesives have the advantage that they do not dry

Fig. 53 A further design based on net print (fig. 50). In this case the various materials which were added were inked up and placed directly on to the net print. For key see fig. 54

Fig. 54 (1) Net shape (2) cut paper shapes (3) woodgrain taken from weathered board (4 & 6) cut cardboard shapes, smaller fish shapes also cut from cardboard (5) leaf shapes. Sky inked up on net base block and printed.

hard, like glue, and therefore make it possible to remove the various shapes after they have been printed, leaving the base block free for further work.

Printing from a base block of this kind presents no great problem, though due to the differences in thickness and character of the materials used, some difficulty may be experienced at first in inking up with the roller. You will find that certain materials, especially fabrics, absorb more ink than others and will therefore require to be inked up rather more heavily. However, once the first prints have been taken and the ink allowed to dry into the block, the ink will form a resist and also act as a binder, preventing any further absorption of ink as well as holding together the looser fibres of these materials which at first will tend to get picked up on the inked roller.

Another point that should be emphasised with regard to the base block method, where the materials are fixed or placed down, is that it can be used in a registration frame in much the same way as a lino or wood block, so making it possible to build up in stages to the final print. Having taken an impression from the first shapes, the print can be lifted, further shapes inked up and placed down relative to these, and the print developed in this way.

When taking a print from a base block, it will be necessary to ensure that all parts of the inked surface are transferred to the paper. This can best be achieved in the following way. Once the block has been satisfactorily inked up, place the printing paper over it, allowing for a suitable margin around the edges. Then, whilst holding the print down firmly with one hand, take a clean roller and roll lightly over the back of the print, working from the centre outwards to ensure that the printing surface is pressed down evenly over the whole area of the block.

Where differences of thickness have to be coped with, it will be found helpful to burnish with a rag made up into a pad, so that pressure may be applied to the lower surfaces of the block. Further burnishing may then be carried out with a harder implement, such as a spoon, over those areas where more solid colour or tone is required, remembering to lift the print occasionally for inspection.

From what I have said regarding the use of a base block, it will be appreciated that a considerable variety of treatment and effect is possible. The majority of the prints which

I have used to illustrate the media were in part produced with a base block, further shapes and textures being added by what I would describe, for want of a better term, as the 'direct method'.

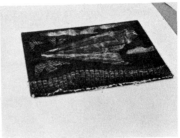

Fig. 55 Arranging materials on base block

Fig. 56 Materials fixed to base block

Fig. 57 Base block shown in registration frame

2 The direct method

Where it is necessary to overprint shapes and textures one over another in order to develop the depth and colour range in a print, this method will prove the only practical way of working.

Here, instead of fixing or placing the materials on to a base as described above, we place them after inking either on to a block or directly on to the printing surface of the paper. Printing shapes in this way permits of complete freedom as regards the order in which the various materials may be printed, and also makes it possible to use colour more widely than with the base block method.

Fig. 58 Cut cardboard, wire gauze, plastic grid and wood grain. All were inked up and positioned before printing on print surface.

This method of working, being direct, means that you do not have to visualise your print in reverse. The image you are printing will come out the same way round as you see it when placed down on the paper.

If you wish, you can use this method solely to produce a print. It will depend very much on the materials used, but it is obvious that by combining the two methods we can more fully exploit the range of our materials; the base block can be used for printing from the more delicate and flexible materials, and the direct method for those that are sufficiently firm and physically large enough to ink up separately and to place down directly on to the printing surface.

Fig. 59 Print taken from glass fragments and plastic netting. Net shape fixed down on base block.

8 Masks and stencils

An example of a mask and of a stencil are shown in fig. 60. The mask is what might be termed the positive shape, that is, cut out from the paper or thin cardboard. The stencil is the negative shape or aperture that is left.

The mask

This is used as the term implies as a means of shielding or covering up an area on a base block in the case of collage printing, after the ink has been applied. The effect will be to leave those areas over which the mask has been placed white, or the colour of the printing paper. Let me illustrate this more fully with a simple example, as shown in fig. 61. Here the base block (a piece of hardboard) was inked up with blue printing ink. A series of diamond shapes were then cut out of paper and placed down on to the inked surface. A print was then taken. As a further means of developing the pattern, a number of rectangles were cut out, and after removing the original shapes, the block was then inked up in orange and the final print taken. Although it was not possible to show the print in colour, the different tones

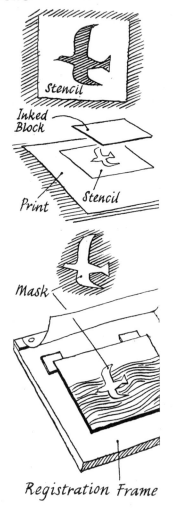

Fig. 60 Masks and stencils

Fig. 61 Simple print produced with the use of masks. The diamond shapes were first placed down on a piece of hardboard inked up with blue and a print taken. The base block was then cleaned and re-inked with orange and masked off with paper squares. A further print was then taken.

show that there are four distinct values = the white of the paper, blue, orange and the overprinting of the two colours as a purple grey. This use of masks is most effective when used with a base block, as the inked surface of the block serves as a means of holding the thin paper or cardboard shapes in position.

The same result may however be achieved with the use of masks when employing the free or direct method of printing. In this case, the mask is placed down on to the print itself, and the surface texture required to print is inked up, placed over it and burnished in the normal way. You will see that by using the mask in this way, you can achieve the same effect by reversing the position of the inked surface. In the case of the base block the ink lies underneath the mask, but when using the direct method, the inked surface is applied over the mask.

57

Before dealing with the use of the stencil, one further point remains to be said with regard to the mask. Apart from its use as a means of creating shapes within a collage design, it is also of service when areas of textured materials, or shapes that have been cut, extend outside the print itself and therefore require to be masked off before printing. Strips of paper of a suitable width may be used around the printing area for this purpose.

The stencil

This is the negative shape which, like its counterpart the mask, is used as a means of controlling tone or colour.

Fig. 62 shows an example of a pattern produced in this way with a simple stencil. It will be seen that the stencil permits the textures used to print only within the area of the cut out. Unlike the mask, it has a rather more restricted use, being applied only in the direct way to the surface of the print, the textured surface to be printed being placed down over it.

A particular advantage of the stencil is that it makes it possible to take an impression from the surface of materials without having to cut them to the particular shape, a useful expedient in cases where the materials are of a hard nature, e.g. metal, hardwood, glass, plastic, etc.

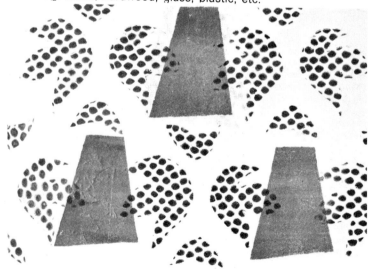

Fig. 62 Print produced with the use of cut stencils.

Fig. 63 Monotype print. Free drawing on glass with brush. Parts then worked on with soft rag, palette knife and shaped stick.

9 Monotype

This is a medium which differs from the relief methods described in that the design is drawn by various means directly on to the flat surface of a suitably non-absorbent material, such as glass, hardboard, metal or plastic sheeting, etc., and the image transferred by placing a sheet of paper over it and applying pressure. Though less easily controlled compared with the cut design, the freedom and spontaneity of treatment that it permits is much akin to that of the painter.

The design may be effected in a number of ways: -

(a) Using a brush, drawing can be done directly on the surface using as many colours as one chooses. With the use of a rag and various shaped wood or metal tools, which can be improvised for the purpose, parts of the colour can

Fig. 64 Inked surface of glass

Fig. 65 Marks made with rag and various shaped tools

Fig. 66 Masks laid over inked surface

be removed or dragged in different ways to produce lines, tones and textural effects. A sheet of paper can then be laid over it, and with the use of a rag pad and roller, the ink transferred to it. (See fig. 65.)

(b) The plate rolled up with a single colour or a number of colours, further drawing being done with the brush, the rag and tools.

(c) A similar technique employed as in (b), but with the addition of torn or cut paper shapes used as masks and placed down after the drawing has been done, to produce areas of white in the print. (See fig. 66.)

(d) A further method of producing a print using monotype is to roll up or paint the block in a single colour or a number of colours. Then place a sheet of paper over it, and with the use of a flat or pointed tool - the end of a paint brush or shaped stick - draw freely upon the surface of the paper. When removed, it will be found that the ink will have been transferred to the print only in those parts where the pressure has been applied, the remaining areas of the paper showing white.

Fig. 67 Monotype print. Ink applied with roller. Further drawing done with rag, palette knife, etc.

If required, a guide to the design can be made first on a sheet of paper, which is then placed under a sheet of glass so that the lines can be clearly seen through. Colour is applied to the glass with a brush or roller. If the drawing underneath has been done in ink or black crayon, it will clearly show through the colour, areas of which can then be removed with the rag and tools to print up white where required.

Although registration need not be considered seriously when using a medium of this nature, a simple means of fixing the printing paper to the glass can be found by hinging the printing paper on the top with two strips of gummed paper or Scotch tape. With the paper fixed in this manner the print

61

Fig. 68 Monotype print. Colours applied with brush and roller. Sail shapes masked off and further drawing done with tools before printing.

can be built up in stages, wiping the surface of the glass clean between the printing and drawing stages. Alternatively the registration frame can be used.

It will be seen from the few examples of treatment described, that the effects that it is possible to achieve in the medium are extremely wide, especially when the different techniques of applying the colour are combined. Any type of oil or watercolour ink or paint may be used, and different effects experimented with by using it in varying consistencies. When using oil colour, turps substitute can be splashed on the colour before printing to produce very interesting results.

The term given to this form of print making implies that it is only intended for the production of a single print, but although strictly speaking this is true, as no two identical prints can be got from the same design, it is possible to take more than one print from the surface providing a sufficient surplus of ink remains.

Care of tools and equipment

When you have completed work for the day, it is important to give thought to your tools and printing equipment. Rollers should be thoroughly cleaned by firstly removing the excess ink by rolling them over a sheet of newspaper, finishing off with turpsy rags if oil-based inks have been used, or damp rags for water-based inks. If a simply constructed stand can be made as shown in fig. 10, and the rollers placed in it when not in use, it will help protect them and extend their life.

The inking slabs and palette knives must be similarly cleaned with turps substitute or water according to the nature of the inks used, making sure to dry the palette knives carefully if water is used.

All cutting tools should be carefully placed in a rollup type bag as shown in fig. 11, or in a suitable piece of soft material. A little machine oil should be smeared on them if they are to be left for any length of time without being used.

The surface of colour blocks should be wiped clear of ink with a turpsy rag or water before being put away.

Fig. 69 A screen print from paper shapes

Fig. 70 French chalk was used as a resist in making this print

Screen printing

Screen printing, which is essentially a stencilling craft, has been adapted over the years to suit the needs of contemporary printers. The term 'a screen print' is widely used and refers to printed decoration on a variety of materials and goods.

Early stencil impressions found in caves and believed to be many thousands of years old are examples of man's desire to decorate his surroundings. From such simple beginings, stencil methods used in screen printing have been developed. Today, our homes are decorated with screen printed wallpaper, fabrics, tiles and pottery. Many large posters, showcards and general advertising matter, together with cartons and other containers, are printed by this process.

The production of pictorial prints, employing screen printing techniques adapted to the needs of the craft worker, will be fully described, and well tried methods suitable for the beginner and widely used in schools today to reproduce students' work should be well within the capabilities of the interested reader. Instructions will be kept as simple as possible and, if followed step by step, are not complicated. A trial and error period is inevitable with any craft, but this should not deter the inexperienced amateur who will soon produce stimulating results.

Equipment, tools and materials are kept to a minimum. Once the basic technique has been tried and first results produced, you may like to invest in more elaborate equipment. A note of stockists of specialist supplies to screen printers, where helpful advice is available, can be found on p. 95.

The general principle is that shapes are cut or torn from paper to form a design or pattern, which is then applied to a tightly stretched mesh. Ink is forced through the cut out areas of the stencil and through the mesh, transferring the design to paper placed under the mesh. Screen printing differs from the other stencil printing methods already described. Ink is never applied direct to the stencil, but is passed through the fine mesh or screen to which the stencil carrying the design in the form of cut out shapes is attached. The mesh in turn is fixed to a rigid frame that is hinged to a baseboard. A strip of rubber called a squeegee is used to force the ink through the open mesh areas of the stencil on to paper placed on the baseboard under the frame, so transferring the stencil image to the paper or chosen printing surface. Any number of prints may be made on separate sheets of paper from the same stencil.

You will realise that a stencil forms the basis of this printing craft. It can be of paper or other substance that will resist ink and prevent it penetrating areas of the mesh that do not form part of the design. Glue and French (powdered) chalk both fulfill this requirement and make good resists. These and other methods of stencil making will be fully described. Simple stencils are made quickly, and the beginner with a feeling for line and colour but with little drawing ability will find, in making such stencils, scope to develop these talents. After initial trials from which good results should be achieved with little skill, you will be encouraged to experiment with other stencil mediums.

It is possible to produce prints on a variety of surfaces - paper, cardboard, hardboard, wood. The texture of the printing surface, if carefully chosen, can form part of the design. Examples of such surfaces are given, but the choice is limitless, and it is up to the imaginative reader to develop designs to include these textures.

Production of prints in two, three or more colours is possible, and if the instructions given are followed carefully, good results should be obtained.

10 Equipment and materials

The following are the basic requirements needed to make a start. Many of the items are in everyday use and can easily be gathered together; these are listed first (fig. 79): -
Pair of large sharp scissors; screwdriver; soft pencil, grade 'B'; drawing pins (thumbtacks) or a small stapling punch; pair of pliers; gummed paper tape 1" wide; 12" rule, metal if possible; a supply of soft rag and newspaper for cleaning purposes. In addition, the following items will require to be specially purchased or made.

Fig. 71

Fig. 72

(a) The frame and base

A suitable size to start with is 20" x 12". These are the inside measurements, but much will depend on individual requirements and the material to be printed. For a start, a strong picture frame could be used. If specially constructed, the timber should be at least 2" x 1" and have strong corner joints made with glue and screws. The wood should be smooth, and the edges rounded with sandpaper and finished with a coat of varnish. The base can be a table top or separate board; blockboard is ideal for the purpose. Strong brass

Fig. 73

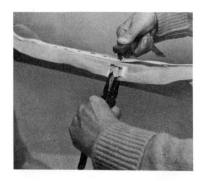

Fig. 74

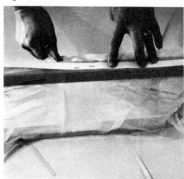

Fig. 75

Fig. 76

hinges and screws are needed to secure the frame to the baseboard. Make a prop arm from a short piece of wood, and screw to side of frame as illustrated in fig. 71.

(b) Organdie

The material for the mesh should have a fairly close weave. Organdie, a cotton material, usually white, which may be purchased in various widths from many drapery (fabric) stores, is ideal and reasonably priced, and is recommended for the beginner. To stretch the organdie mesh over the frame, follow these instructions carefully as it needs to be as tightly and evenly stretched as possible to avoid distortion in the final printing. When the frame is completely covered, the mesh should be drum tight. A helping hand is needed if this is to be achieved, as the mesh must be under tension while being fixed to the frame. A pair of pliers is helpful for stretching the mesh during fixing, but the jaws should be protected by cardboard or felt to prevent any damage to the mesh (fig. 74). Cut a piece of organdie 4″ overall larger than the frame, that is, 28″ x 20″ for the frame size given. Four strips of cardboard $\frac{1}{2}$″ wide are needed, one for each of the short and long edges. Have ready a box of drawing pins (thumbtacks) or a small stapling punch. Make a fold of $1\frac{1}{2}''$ on one short side of the mesh and place this over the corresponding edge of the frame, allowing it to overhang the frame by about $\frac{3}{4}''$. Now take a short strip of the cardboard and place it over the mesh on the edge of the frame and fix both in position in the centre. Continue in this way, completing a centre section of about one third of the length, placing pins or staples at $1''$ intervals as shown in fig. 75. Now, stretching the mesh with the pliers, work on side 2 and fix a centre section as previously described. Work round the frame in this way, following the diagram numbers for the order of fixing and folding the mesh and leaving a piece overhanging to grip on all sides (fig. 77). Place strips of cardboard which may be glued for added strength between the mesh and fixing, finishing corners neatly with extra pins and trimming off the surplus material when the stretching has been completed.

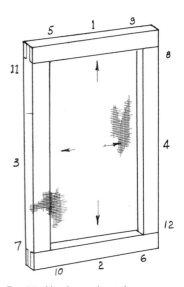

Fig. 77 Numbers show the order of stretching organdie over frame

(c) Squeegee (fig. 78)

This is uséd to force ink through the mesh and is most suitable if it consists of a wooden handle into which is set a strip of hard rubber $\frac{1}{4}''$ thick

Fig. 78

and $1\frac{1}{2}''$ wide. Alternatively, the handle may be in two parts with the rubber sandwiched between and projecting, so that the sharp square edges can be used. A sandpaper block is useful to sharpen squeegee rubber when it becomes rounded at the edges. Manufactured squeegees are available, but a trial may be made with a homemade one using rubber draught excluder strip, but this will only have a short life. A suitable size squeegee for the frame described is $11''$, or $1''$ less than the inside frame measurement.

(d) Stencil knife (fig. 80)

Craft knives have sharp fine blades suitable for stencil cutting purposes. An oilstone is a useful item for keeping the blade sharp and in good condition. Stencil knives are available from specialist suppliers.

(e) Inks

Oil-bound poster inks are recommended as they do not clog the organdie mesh and are quick drying. Supplied in a wide range of intermixable colours and thinned with turps substitute, they dry with a slight sheen and can be used on most surfaces, including paper, cardboard and wood. Flexible inks that do not need after treatment, and are semi-permanent, are available for fabric printing, if you want the fabric to be washable.

(f) A drying rack (fig. 96)

This should be prepared before commencing to print. A clothes line or clothes airer and clothes pegs is most effective and prints may be hung back to back in pairs, allowing air to circulate between them and so speed the drying time. Most surfaces printed with the recommended inks will dry within an hour.

(g) 4" palette knife (fig. 79)

This is the best tool for stirring and mixing ink, and is used for scraping surplus ink from the screen mesh when printing is finished.
Sundry items are also needed: -
A pair of brass hinges $2''$ to $3''$ with suitable screws for fixing to base board. Turps substitute for cleaning and

thining - about ½″ gallon should be purchased in the first instance. A bottle of liquid glue or gum, 8 oz. size. Brushes - Nos. 1 and 3 sable paint brushes and ½″ house painter's brush. ½ doz. large, black, wax crayons as used for package marking. ½ lb. French (powdered) chalk.

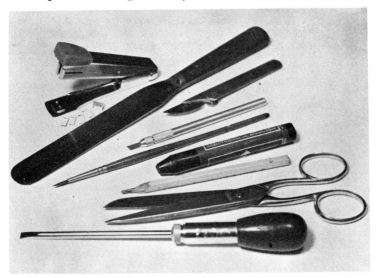

Fig. 79 Some of the necessary tools. From the top down: stapler, palette knife, two stencil knives, fine pointed brush, wax crayon, pencil, scissors and screwdriver

11 Stencil making methods

It is now time to explore the various methods of making a stencil. A start should be made with paper stencils as they are the easiest and quickest to make, and can be used in many different ways.

You need a sheet of paper large enough to cover the frame area, i.e., 20″ x 12″ if the recommended frame size has been used. Paper that is not too absorbent is best. The kind used to make paper bags and known as sulphite paper is ideal, as it has a surface that resists ink and is easily cut with a craft or stencil knife. Any thin paper, such as brown wrapping, greaseproof paper or even a sheet of newspaper, may be used for a first trial.

Mark out an area 14″ x 9″ in the centre of the sheet of paper. Within this area cut or tear a series of shapes to form the design. As a first experiment, if you do not want to tackle drawing, a collection of small objects - bottles, cans, cotton reels (spools), coins, etc. - are useful for drawing round, and if placed in an interesting way on the paper, can form the basis of a repeat pattern.

Now determine the areas to be cut out by marking with a pencil, remembering that these are the parts of the design that will appear in colour on the final print. Take the stencil knife, which should be held as a pen, and cut round the pencilled outlines. Try to make long, continuous cuts with the knife to avoid an irregular outline; a little practice will determine the correct amount of pressure necessary to make a clean cut. When complete, the stencil will appear as a series of holes with an outer margin of paper (fig. 81). This margin is always necessary to allow squeegee movement on the frame and to prevent ink penetrating unwanted areas of the stencil. Whatever size frame is used, the stencil area should always be at least 6″ x 3″ smaller than the inside frame measurements. The stencil printing area can, of course, be much less if the chosen design is contained in a correspondingly small area.

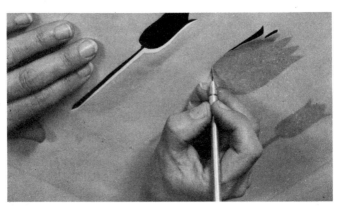

Fig. 80

The cut out stencil is now ready to be attached to the mesh. Raise the frame and with small pieces of gummed paper or Scotch tape stick the stencil by the corners to the underside of the organdie mesh, keeping it as flat and even as possible. Where areas of paper tend to curl away from the mesh, they may be held in place by small dabs of liquid glue brushed over the stencil paper on the mesh side (fig. 81). The stencil is now ready for printing.

Fig. 81

Now select your printing paper, which should be at least 1" larger overall than the stencil area, 15" x 10" in the case of the stencil described. This margin allows for handling the print when wet and can later be trimmed off if desired. Place the paper on the baseboard. Determine the right position by measuring 3" in from long side of frame and 4½" in from short side, clearly marking these measurements on the baseboard. These measurements are the difference between the outside frame size and the printing paper size, when standard frame measurements and 2" x 1" timber are used, and should be varied according to the frame and timber actually used. The marks on the baseboard are known as register guides, and if only one print is being made, the printing paper should be lined up with these guide marks.

Fig. 82

Fig. 83

Fig. 84 Wax impression of flower with over print using paper shapes and translucent ink

Fig. 85 An impression of hessian (burlap) overprinted with paper shapes and dripped and translucent inks

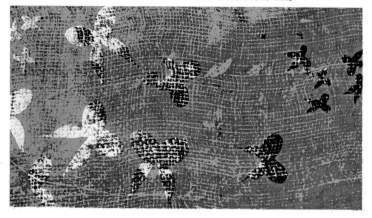

Fig. 86 Similar print from same stencil

Fig. 87 French chalk drawn in with a comb produced the windmill

Fig. 88 Tulips from paper stencil printed with translucent inks

Fig. 89 Paper shapes and dripped and translucent inks

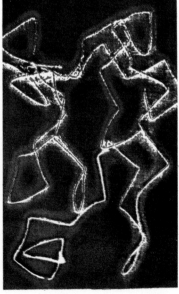

Fig. 90 String was used to give the impression of dancing figures

If, however, you intend to make a series of prints from the same stencil, more accurate register guides are necessary and should be made from gummed paper in the following way. Fold one inch of the strip in half and half again. Then open this out and stick the centre fold together so that a hinged flap is formed. Stick the remaining gummed edges to the baseboard in line with the register guides already made. The printing paper can now be located under these flaps. Three of these register guides are necessary to hold the paper in the correct position, and it is best to put two on the long side at the left and one on the short side slightly to left of centre (fig. 83).

12 Printing

Having prepared the screen, you are now ready to make a print. Your ink, thinned with turps to the consistency of cream, should be free from lumps. It is best to make up a small quantity in a separate container; any ink left over after printing can be returned to the original tin. With the frame lowered on to the baseboard, pour a long pool of ink across the frame at the hinged end. Now hold the squeegee firmly with both hands at an angle on one of the sharp edges and, keeping this angle, pull the ink with a firm even stroke across the mesh.

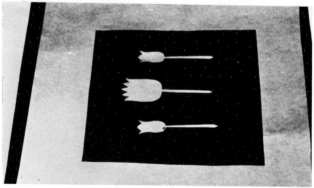

Fig. 91

Fig. 92

Fig. 93

Fig. 94

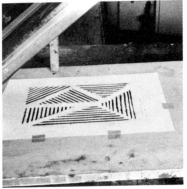

Fig. 95

Fig. 92 shows the angle and method of holding the squeegee. In fig. 93 the pool of ink can be seen on the mesh, and in fig. 94 the squeegee is at the other end of the frame, the pull having been made. Fig. 95 shows the frame in the raised position and the final print in the register guides on the baseboard.

Raise the frame, carefully take off the print and peg it up to dry by the outer margin on the prepared drying line. You will soon discover just how much ink to allow after the first pull. Place a second sheet of paper in the register guides, lower the frame and repeat the process for further prints from the same stencil.

If a number of prints are to be made, work as quickly as possible to keep the ink flowing. It is as well to have one person to pull the squeegee and a second person to place the paper in the register guides and to remove the print for drying. However, when working alone, keep the hands as clean and as free from ink as possible, so that prints are not marked by handling.

Prints hung in a current of air take only 20 to 30 mins to dry. It can prove interesting to replace one of these prints on the baseboard, this time not in the register guides but slightly to the left or right of the original position. Lower the frame and make another pull, thus obtaining a variety of effects from the same stencil (fig. 101).

Further experiments may be made at this stage. Drip inks of various colours on the mesh and squeegee them across at the same time, moving the squeegee slightly from side to side to give an interesting distribution of colour. Trial prints made from the same stencil and without cleaning up between ink changes will give multicolour effects (figs. 86-90).

When the desired number of prints have been made, clean up as quickly as possible (fig. 97). Surplus ink should first

Fig. 96

be scraped from the mesh and the squeegee with the palette knife. This ink can be saved and reused if placed in an airtight container, or returned to the original can, remembering always to replace the lid tightly. A little turps poured on top of the ink will help to keep it in good condition for future use. Now remove the unwanted stencil. Place sheets of newspaper on the baseboard, lower the frame and pour a small quantity of turps over the mesh. Then, with a soft rag, clean until all trace of ink has been removed, replacing rag and newspapers and using more turps as necessary. Dry with a clean rag, removing all trace of ink and turps and leaving the mesh area clear when held up to the light. The screen is now ready to be reused. If this cleaning process is carried out after printing from any type of stencil, the organdie mesh will have a reasonably long life. Palette knives and squeegees should be cleaned with turps after use and ink not allowed to dry hard on the tools. Follow these simple cleaning rules to keep the equipment in good condition.

Other methods of using paper stencils should be tried. Prints made from the stencil just described will have the design area appearing in colour. It is possible to make a reverse print where the background is coloured (fig. 91). On a sheet of 20″ x 12″ paper, mark in the centre an oblong 14″ x 9″. Now with scissors or a craft knife, cut round this area, retaining the outer paper frame and discarding the 14″ x 9″ centre shape. Attach this frame of paper to the

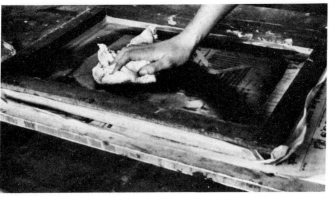

Fig. 97

underside of the mesh in the same way as for the first stencil, by pieces of tape at the corner. Now cut out from another sheet of paper a series of shapes to form the stencil. Raise the frame and lay them in an interesting position on the baseboard; lower the frame and brush a little glue over the paper shapes through the mesh, allowing the glue to dry; raise the frame and the stencil shapes will be in position on the mesh. Prints may now be made as previously described. You will now find that the background area is printed in colour, the design being formed by the unprinted areas of paper (fig. 69).

Experiment by overprinting some of the earlier prints with the reverse stencil. Exciting results may be achieved if ink of a different colour is used, and a variety of interesting prints can be produced (fig. 100).

Overprinting with translucent inks can lead to a variety of experiments. Ink is made translucent or transparent by the addition of a substance known as translucent base. To mix such ink, take a small quantity of the base and add to it a very small amount of the chosen colour ink in the proportion of about one part ink to four of base. When mixed together with turps to the normal creamy consistency, a clear transparent colour will be produced. Greater or lesser degrees of transparency may be made by varying the proportions of base to ink. Always start with the base and add the colour to it, never the other way round, to avoid waste of base.

These methods will produce a design in a single colour, second colours being produced by overprinting or by printing with a variety of coloured or translucent ink. To produce sections of a design in different colours, make a separate stencil for each colour, e.g., red flowers and green leaves need two stencils, all the red parts to be cut from one stencil and the green from another. A master drawing indicating the coloured areas must be made to work from, and the stencil paper placed over the drawing when cutting the stencils. In order that the two stencils will print in the correct position or register, the following method must be used. Mark a cross at the bottom left and right-hand sides of the original drawing, and cut these crosses with the red and then with the green stencil. Now place one stencil over the other with crosses together, and see that the two stencils do in fact fit together. With this method of registration it is possible with care to make prints from one original with

Fig. 98 A print from the stencil shown in fig. 91

Fig. 99 The stencil in fig. 91 was used with translucent ink and overprinted on the black part to give a second impression

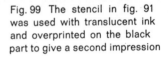

Fig. 100 The print has been moved and the colour changed

Fig. 101 Three colour printing using translucent inks and moving the print

four, five or even more colours, but great care must be taken to produce a good coloured original complete with register crosses, which must appear cut out on each stencil.

Make the prints in the way already described for single colour printing, but make sure that the crosses appear on the print margin. After the first colour has been printed, it is a simple matter, when the second stencil is on the mesh, to lower the frame and match up the crosses by moving the print on the baseboard until the two sets of crosses correspond. The second colour will then print in absolute register with the first. By putting gummed paper register guides as before, you will be able to place the paper in the correct position on the baseboard.

13   Resist stencils

A resist type stencil made with French (powdered) chalk has only a short life and is better used for experimental purposes. No master drawing is necessary, and this allows greater freedom to explore the possibilities of the medium, as much is left to one's ingenuity. The general principles are described and you will realise that they open up a wide field.

A piece of black or other dark coloured paper should be placed on the baseboard, the frame hinged to the board being left in the raised position. Sprinkle French chalk on to this paper. A can with holes punched in the bottom and filled with the chalk is useful for getting an even distribution of the chalk. The paper should be lightly covered all over

Fig. 102

the area forming the design, which should not be larger than the usual printing size of 14" x 9". Surplus chalk outside this area may be left to form a block out, and may then extend to cover the whole area of the frame; in this way, no masking out will be necessary.

When the paper is covered by the thin layer of chalk, draw with a finger in the chalk to form a pattern. You will find that the chalk has been pushed to one side and areas of the dark paper will be left showing, if sufficient chalk has been sprinkled. It is difficult to say just how much chalk is needed, but the best description is enough to form a slight ridge when it is drawn in

Printing is now carried out in the normal way. Pour a pool of ink across the mesh and squeegee this across; raise the frame carefully without knocking it and peel away the paper so as not to disturb the chalk, which will now be found adhering to the mesh with the ink. Place printing paper on the baseboard, lower the frame and make a further print. When peeled carefully off the mesh, you will see a true reproduction of the chalk drawing if sufficient chalk was sprinkled on the dark paper. Should ink have penetrated unwanted design areas, insufficient chalk has been used. A little chalk may come away with the first print if too much has been used, but it will shake off the print

Fig. 103 Masked section of lace curtaining

Fig. 104 Sprinkled with French chalk

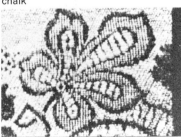

Fig. 105 Lace removed leaving chalk impression

79

Another method is to place on the dark paper a piece of material such as patterned lace curtaining, crochet work or other material having an open weave with or without a pattern. Sprinkle the chalk all over the material, making sure that open areas are covered with a layer of chalk. Now carefully lift off the material so that the impression is not disturbed. Lower the frame and make a print, being sure to allow sufficient ink to cover the whole patterned area of the mesh so that the chalk will adhere to it. Peel away the print carefully and a faithful reproduction of the material should result. At least ten prints can usually be made by working quickly and taking care not to smudge the chalk. Other methods of reproducing the design or pattern in the chalk are by drawing with or dragging a comb, fork or coarse bristle brush to give texture impressions.

Cut paper shapes placed on the paper before the French chalk, and left when the frame is lowered and the first pull made, are another way of combining two methods. Shapes should be fairly small and they will then adhere to the ink with the chalk and produce results similar to those in fig. 110, which was produced from a combination of net curtain and paper shapes. Small objects with distinctive outline can be impressed into the chalk, but they should be removed with care. A pair of tweezers will be found helpful, as in this way the impression will not be disturbed.

Fig. 106

Fig. 107

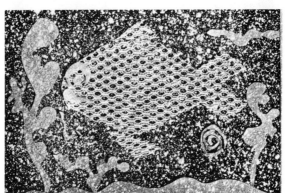

Fig. 108

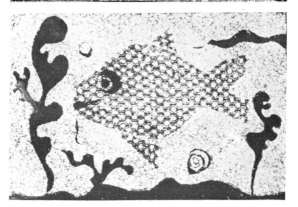

Fig. 109

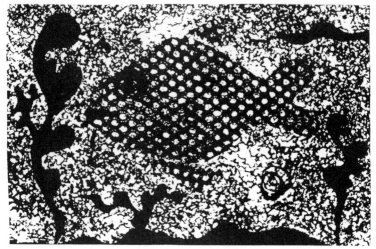

Fig. 110 The final print after the stages shown on p. 81. Areas shown as white are imprinted and remain the colour of the paper. Colour appears in black areas, clearly showing the outline of the paper shapes and net.

Sand may be used in a similar way. It should be sprinkled on the paper sparingly, being heavier than the chalk. A little may fall on the final print, but this may even help to add interest to the design (fig. 106).

With this type of resist stencil, it is not possible to wash off the ink and use another colour, as this would also remove the chalk which is held in position by the ink. Other colours may be incorporated by dripping areas of colour on to the mesh, or by adding other colours to the pool of ink and squeegeeing them across together to give a multi-coloured print.

After printing, clean with turps. This will also remove the French chalk so that only one cleaning operation is necessary. A little more turps than usual may be needed to clean the mesh completely.

Crayon resist stencil

Another type of resist stencil can be made with wax crayon and glue. This method can be used to reproduce many textured surfaces such as grainy wood, sandpaper in a number of different grades, the reverse side of hardboard and many woven surfaces. Exciting prints may be made without the need to produce a design or drawing first, and this can be a great encouragement to the beginner. Reproductions of rubbings of relief sculpture, church brasses, wood carving, inscriptions from ancient tombstones are all suitable subjects for prints made from this type of stencil.

The basic method is as follows: –

Areas of design to be printed are blocked out directly on to the mesh by rubbing over with the wax crayon. Glue is then poured over the whole area of the mesh, filling all non-printing areas, and the waxed portions resist the penetration of the glue. When the glue is dry, the wax crayon is removed with turps, leaving areas of open mesh for the ink to pass through. Experiments may first be made by placing paper over a variety of surfaces and rubbing with the crayon to transfer the impression to the paper. You will quickly discover just how much pressure is needed. It is sometimes better to use the crayon on one side, or the flat end rather than the sharpened point, to get good results.

When making this type of stencil it is better to have the screen free from the baseboard, and it will of course be necessary, when reproducing church brasses, stone reliefs, etc., to take the screen to the chosen surface to make the wax impression. Other surfaces may be placed on the baseboard for this part of the process.

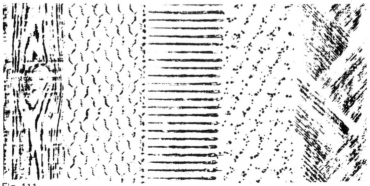

Fig. 111

Fig. 112

Fig. 113

Fig. 114

When making the wax crayon impression on the mesh, press hard enough to ensure that the mesh is completely filled with the wax. Check that a good impression has been transferred by holding the frame up to the light. Pinholes letting light through need filling with more crayon.

When all parts of the design to be printed appear as areas of solid black crayon on the mesh, it is ready to receive a coating of glue filler (fig. 116). Raise the frame at one end by propping it up a few inches with a block of wood. This is necessary to prevent glue dripping through the back of the mesh and to assist the flow of the glue (fig. 116). Pour a little glue across the raised end of the screen, and with a piece of stiffish cardboard, spread it in a thin even coat over the mesh. Work quickly to get the glue on evenly over the whole area without allowing it to drip through the back. Spread it in one direction at first then, adding more glue, work it over the mesh at right angles, keeping a thin even coat of glue. In this way, pinholes in the glued areas will be avoided (fig. 117).

Now leave the glue to dry. After about ten minutes a fan type heater may be used to speed this process, but it should be placed several feet away from the screen, to avoid drying the glue too quickly thus causing it to crack. The next stage is to remove the wax crayon. Take care to ensure that the glue is completely dry before attempting this stage of the process. Spread newspaper under the frame, pour a generous amount of turps over the screen and leave it to soak for a few moments. The turps will dissolve the wax which can now be removed by rubbing both sides of the screen with a soft turps-soaked rag, taking care not to press too hard on the mesh. As the rag becomes blackened with wax, replace it, finally drying the mesh with a clean rag. Now hold the frame up to the light to check for pinholes in the glue. These can quickly be blocked out with a fine brush dipped in glue. The stencil is now ready for printing. This type of stencil is long lasting. It can be used to make any number of prints, and can be cleaned down if colour changes are required.

These illustrations show stages in making a wax impression on mesh. The glue process is show in figs 116-7.

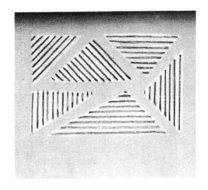

Fig. 115

Fig. 116

Fig. 117

After first trial prints made from this type of stencil, look around for other textured surfaces to reproduce. Wood block floors and many varieties of glass have interesting surfaces (fig. 111). Designs may be built up by using a number of different textures and it is possible, with care, to reproduce veined leaves, grasses in flower, feathers and other natural forms (fig. 122).

Fig. 118 Wax impression of a manhole cover made directly on to the mesh used to produce the print above

14 Printing from natural forms

There are a variety of ways in which pressed leaves, grasses, flowers and even feathers can be incorporated in the designs for screen prints. Negative prints may be made which will produce only the outline of the specimens on a printed ground. Second printings or overprintings with cut paper stencils to produce positive prints will give striking results if translucent inks are used and if a little thought is given to the arrangement of the forms (fig. 119).

It is a good idea to start a scrap book in which to collect specimens that may be found from time to time. In this way they will be preserved undamaged and pressed flat until ready for use. A library of specimens may be built up containing natural forms like those already mentioned. Choose specimens that have a distinctive outline, such as oak, sycamore and chestnut leaves. Grasses are best gathered in full flower; feathers should be fairly small and the quills hammered flat to avoid damage to the mesh. Man-made textured materials can also be included, such as a variety of grades of sandpaper, embossed wallpaper and material with an interesting weave such as canvas, hessian (burlap) and similar textured surfaces. These, together with shells and tree bark, may be used when making a collage type print from crayon resist stencils.

Printing from leaves, grasses or flowers

The first step is to cut a paper mask to contain the printing area. From a sheet of sulphite or brown paper large enough to cover the whole area of the frame, mark out in the centre an oblong 14″ x 9″. Cut this oblong of paper away and stick the remaining paper shape to the underside of the frame with small pieces of gummed paper at each corner.

Now with the frame in the raised position, place on the baseboard another sheet of paper with the same area marked out. This time do not cut the oblong away, but use this space to contain the design by placing the chosen specimens within the area. Arrange the leaves, grasses, etc. remembering that the background area will print in colour and the leaves, etc. will remain the colour of the printing paper (fig. 119).

Fig. 119 Grasses and leaves glued to the mesh give a printed background with the specimens reproduced in the white areas

When you are satisfied that the best arrangement of the specimens has been made, lower the mask-covered frame and with care move the paper on the baseboard until the outlined area lines up with the cut out mask on the frame.

At this stage, if any of the specimens are large and therefore heavy, take a fine brush dipped in glue and dab small spots of glue at the tips and centre of leaves, etc. that may not otherwise adhere to the ink when it is squeegeed across the mesh. When the glue is almost dry, place a sheet of paper over the mesh and apply pressure with the palms of the hands over the glued areas. Remove the paper and allow the glue to dry completely.

Fig. 120 Print made by placing inked specimens on printing paper under the mesh and overprinting. Wet print blotted to show mesh texture.

Printing is now carried out in the usual way. Choose the ink and use it a little thicker than previously recommended. This will ensure that the specimens will stick to it. Pour a pool of ink on to the mesh at the hinged end of the frame; a fairly large quantity may be required to ensure that the whole printing area is completely printed. After the first pull and before raising the frame, make sure that this has been achieved and that the design area is in fact inked all over. Pour on more ink and make a second pull if you are not at first satisfied. Too much ink is better than not enough.

Finally raise the frame carefully and remove the paper on the baseboard. The specimens will now be stuck to the mesh. Printing can now continue. Work fairly quickly, placing paper on the baseboard, lowering the frame carefully and replenishing the ink as necessary. To ensure good prints, do not leave the frame in the raised position longer than necessary, otherwise some specimens may tend to peel away from the mesh. Should any be found stuck to the print, leave them until the print is dry, when they can easily be removed.

Printing from natural forms in this way can be a little more difficult than some other methods, but final results when the technique has been mastered will prove well worth the extra time and skill needed.

Fig. 121 Print made by sticking pressed wild flowers to mesh. Background printed in colour, with flowers forming a resist and remaining the colour of the printing paper.

For a first trial print, choose some small leaves, grasses, flowers or even petals that have been well pressed (fig. 121). Do not at first glue the specimens, as some at least will adhere with the ink. This trial print will serve as a guide to further print making from similar materials and will show just which specimens need to be glued to the mesh. Place the specimens on the paper covered baseboard, lower the frame, squeegee a good pool of ink across the mesh. Ink may be thinned after the first pull, as if it is too thick, it will tend to clog the mesh and produce patchy prints. With the ink too thin, the specimens will not be held in position and blurred outlines will result.

Clean after printing in the usual way, first removing the specimens. When the turps has dried out of the mesh, it is a simple matter to remove any glue that may remain with a rag soaked in hot water.

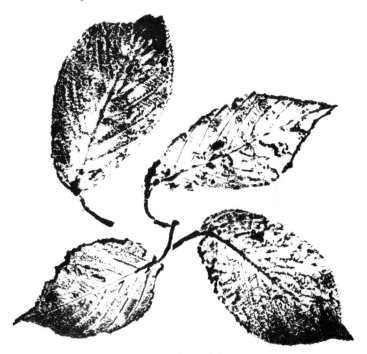

Fig. 122 Print from wax impression of leaves

15 Some general hints

Any time spent on preparation is never time wasted. Gather together all equipment and materials and have them laid out in an orderly fashion, not forgetting newspaper and cleaning rags.

A drying line or rack is a must if more than one or two prints are to be made. Ideally at least six prints should be made from any type of stencil. Once the technique of pulling the squeegee has been perfected, you will realise how quickly prints can be made from any one stencil. Speed in working will always pay off, as the final results will be sharper and cleaner.

Do try to keep hands and equipment free from ink. With a little care and thought, screen printing need not and should not be a messy process. If it is, the basic rules have not been followed. Wear some sort of overall or protective clothing, as accidents will happen.

Always allow plenty of time for clearing up. This includes cleaning mesh, squeegee and knife and removing any stencils from the mesh.

Return any left-over ink to the container and replace the lid to keep the contents airtight and in good condition. Mixed inks should have a little turps poured on top so that a skin will not form. A paper lid is better than none.

A collection of small containers can be very useful for mixing a variety of colours. Prepare more than one colour ink before commencing to print, and have it thinned to the correct consistency.

Have the printing paper in a neat stack on the right and the drying rack on the left if possible. Always cut more paper than required for any given number of prints, until experience has been gained. To save waste of paper, make the first one or two prints on newspaper until you are satisfied with the result.

Another pair of hands is always an asset and a must when stretching the mesh over the frame.

Finally, readers should not restrict themselves to the materials and methods listed here, but should try out their own experiments using the basic techniques set out in this book as a guide.

Paper

Some mention must be made of suitable paper and other printing surfaces relating to the various stencil methods used. Paper of almost any type may be used, from tissue to thick wrapping. If purchased specially, machine glazed or poster paper is recommended. It is stocked by most artists' suppliers in a range of colours and black and white in sheets size 20″ x 30″. This paper has a smooth and a rough side and will print equally well on either surface with any type of stencil. You will notice in the section dealing with stencil making that the printing paper size is given as 10″ x 15″, half the standard sheet size, to avoid waste of paper if it is specially purchased.

Tissue paper takes prints well and is produced in a wide variety of clear bright colours, but it is a little difficult to handle when the prints are wet. Wallpaper and lining paper can be a cheap source of supply and can be cut to a suitable size or printed in the roll. The reverse side of some embossed paper can also be used to good effect.

Papers to be avoided are those with a highly glazed surface, as the normal inks will chip off when dry.

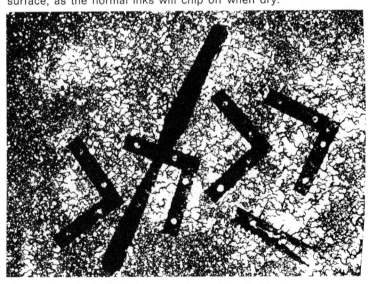

Fig. 123 French chalk used to give the outline of objects

Other printing surfaces

Prints may be made on cardboard, plywood, hessian (burlap), canvas and the reverse side of hardboard, all of which have interesting textured surfaces. French (powdered) chalk stencils are not recommended for these materials, but bold outlines produced by any other stencil method will look well on them, and all will print with the normal oil bound inks.

Fabrics of almost any type - cotton, linen, rayon and silk - are suitable for printing with the special inks. Although it is possible for trial purposes to use the ordinary inks, if the fabric is intended to be washed, semi-permanent flexible inks should be used.

Glass, plastics, tiles and similar surfaces take screen prints well when the correct ink is used, but because of the nature of the surface, normal inks tend to flake off when dry. Those wishing to experiment and make permanent prints should consult the specialist suppliers listed for the correct inks, and drying times should be increased as recommended.

Fig. 124 Left-hand section of print below was made by folding paper in half over wet print on the right to give a reverse print. A paper stencil was used.

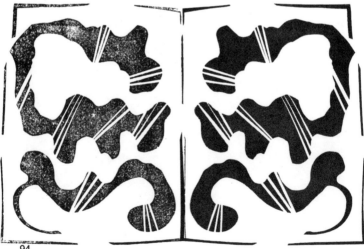

For further reading

Linocuts and Woodcuts by Michael Rothenstein. Studio Vista, London. Watson-Guptill, New York.
Engraving on Wood by J. Farleigh. Dryad, London.
Making Colour Prints by J. Newick. Dryad, London.
Creative Print making by Peter Green. Batsford, London. Published as New Creative Print Making by Watson-Guptill, New York.
Screen Process Printing by Francis Carr. Studio Vista, London.

List of suppliers

Most of the equipment and materials can be obtained from any general art supplier. We have found the following very useful:

Dryad Handicrafts, 22 Bloomsbury St, London, W.C.1.

W. C. Kimber Ltd, 25 Field Street, London, W.C.1.

T. N. Lawrence and Son, 2 Bleeding Heart Yard, Greville St, London, E.C.1.

Winsor & Newton Ltd, 51 Rathbone Place, London, W.1.

In the United States, a great many art and craft supplies can be ordered by mail from Sears, Roebuck, as well as from two large art supply houses which issue mail order catalogs:

Arthur Brown & Bro., 2 West 46th Street, New York, N.Y. 10036

A. I. Friedman, Inc., 25 West 45th Street, New York, N.Y. 10036

Also useful are:

Craftools, Inc., 1 Industrial Rd, Wood-ridge, New Jersey 07075

Graphic Chemical & Ink Co., P.O. Box 27, Villa Park, Ill. 60181

J. Johnson & Co., 51 Manhasset Ave., Manhasset, N.Y. 11030

Specialist suppliers for frames, inks, organdie, squeegees, palette and stencil knives are:

E. T. Marler, 119 Western Rd, Merton Abbey, London, S.W.19

Standard Supply Co., 54 West 21st St, New York, N.Y. 10010

Gibson Paint Co., 1199 East 12th St, Oakland, California 94606

A wide range of coloured papers and cardboard is stocked by:

F. G. Kettle, 127 High Holborn, London, W.1.

Index